Change Ponies,

Other titles by Judith M. Berrisford in Armada

Jackie Won A Pony
Ten Ponies and Jackie
Jackie and the Misfit Pony
Jackie's Pony Patrol
Jackie and the Pony Trekkers
Jackie and the Pony Boys
Jackie's Show Jumping Surprise
Jackie's Pony Camp Summer
Jackie on Pony Island
Jackie and the Pony Thieves
Jackie and the Phantom Ponies
Jackie and the Moonlight Pony
Jackie and the Pony Rivals
Jackie and the Missing Showjumper

CHANGE PONIES, JACKIE!

JUDITH M. BERRISFORD

Illustrated by Geoffrey Whittam

Armada

First published in the U.K. in 1983 by
Hodder & Stoughton Ltd., Sevenoaks.
This edition was first published in Armada
in 1985 by Fontana Paperbacks,
8 Grafton Street, London W1X 3LA.

Printed in Great Britain by
William Collins Sons & Co. Ltd., Glasgow

For Samantha and Jasmine –
Two very special people

CONTENTS

1 *Disaster for Babs*

'Well done, Misty!'

With the second of the practice jumps safely behind us, I slid to the ground to make much of my pony. We were about to compete in the local riding club's cross-country and I wanted Misty to do her best.

'Clever girl.' I slipped my arm over her dappled neck. 'Jump like that on the course and we may well be picked for the team.'

'Lucky you, Jackie!' sighed my cousin, Babs. 'I wish my pony was good enough to stand a chance. It would be wonderful to be chosen to represent Marston in the National Junior Trials.' She tugged at the head of her skewbald, Patch, to prevent him snatching yet another mouthful of grass. 'If only Patch wasn't so fat and greedy I might be picked, too.' She looked me in the eyes. 'Oh, Jackie! I do feel so envious of you and Misty.'

What could I say? It would be glib if I told her to cheer up. How would I feel if I were in her shoes? Fed up, dispirited and, although I'd try hard not to show it, more than a little jealous.

Perhaps I'd been wrong in persuading Babs to enter for the Trials. Patch was always unpredictable. He could jump quite well when he was in the mood but today he obviously wasn't. Already he'd knocked down both of the practice jumps and then obstinately refused to try again. This wasn't one of Patch's jumping days.

'I suppose I'll just have to try to be happy for you, Jackie,' Babs sighed.

'You're a good sport, Babs,' was the only real solace I could honestly give.

Babs was my best friend as well as my cousin. We'd been through so many ups-and-downs together with our ponies. We'd started off by being pony-mad and pony-less, hanging round stables in the hope of a ride. Then we'd each had a stroke of luck which had changed everything.

I'd entered a competition with a pony as first prize – and I'd won! I was allowed to choose my own pony. I'd been about to try out some really showy ponies when I'd seen Misty drawing a firewood cart. [See *Jackie Won a Pony*.]

After days of glory in the show ring, Misty had fallen on hard times. Her over-ambitious young rider had taken a bad fall. The girl's parents had blamed it on Misty and that was how my darling, beloved pony had come to be between those uncomfortable shafts on that eventful day when I'd first seen her.

No sign of her humble fate now remained, except a few whiter-than-usual hairs over the scar that showed just above the fetlock on her off-fore and a sweet, biddable gratitude as if she were for ever thanking me for rescuing her.

Bab's skewbald, Patch, had never known hard times, which is perhaps why he was so wilful and sometimes lazy. He had no need for gratitude. He'd been one of those lucky ponies born to roam the Pony Forest. His mother had been one of Aunt Di's mares which she grazed in the Forest. Aunt Di had trained him and backed him, giving him to Babs on one of our holidays at her Pony Forest cottage. [See *Jackie's Pony Patrol.*]

A sudden bustle at the officials' table cut short any further reflections, and the jostling gathering of ponies, riders, parents, spectators and friends went quiet.

'Number Four on to the course, please,' blared the

loudspeaker. 'Number Four! Miss Barbara Ariadne Bettina Spencer.'

'That's me! Oh, gosh!' Babs gasped in alarm, jamming her crash cap over her chestnut curls and flipping the elastic under her chin before pulling Patch's reins over his head and jumping into the saddle.

I led Misty to the railings to watch as my cousin legged her ever-reluctant skewbald towards the start of the Trials course.

Today, there was an air of tension that was rare in the usually informal, happy-go-lucky proceedings of the Marston-near-the-Sea Riding Club. This year the Club officials had decided to enter a junior team for the National Trials and here were all the Under-Fourteens, hoping to be among the chosen four.

The course was similar to the kind that we would have to face in the National Heats, a mixture of natural and made-up obstacles. The time factor was to be taken into account in reaching a decision, just as it would be in the actual competition. The selectors would be looking for handiness, speed, courage and co-ordination on the part of pony and rider.

Well, there was nothing wrong with Patch's courage or Babs' determination and, as soon as my cousin had heeled the skewbald from his apathy, they set off for the first jump at a game canter.

The obstacle was an easy one, made of brushwood, and Babs and Patch took it in their stride. The second would be a different matter, I knew. I had walked the course with my cousin beforehand and we had both noted the awkward ditch on the landing side of a formidable double-oxer. Standing on the rails now and craning to see how Babs might fare I crossed my fingers for luck.

Patch came at the jump too fast. I saw Babs dig her heels into his sides and urge him to put in an extra stride before take-off.

That extra stride was the skewbald's undoing. It brought him too close to the fence so that he rose almost vertically in a way that would not give him enough scope to clear the spread.

Patch seemed to hesitate in mid-air as he saw the dark ditch yawning before his feet. He kicked out to give himself extra momentum. Taken by surprise Babs was thrown on to his neck.

Her weight brought Patch's head down so that his forefeet struck the ground with a jar. His hind legs slid backwards into the ditch. Babs slipped under his neck and hung there for a moment. Then, with an acrobatic effort, she managed to wriggle on to Patch's withers and to regain her saddle.

Striving to make up lost time, Babs galloped round the bend in the course and headed for the second double-oxer. She came too fast at the jump. Patch realised it and tried to slow down, but Babs, thinking, no doubt, of the seconds ticking steadily away on the selector's clock, gave him a cut with her switch.

That was too much for Patch. He must have realised that, uncollected as he was, he had no hope of getting over the jump. Sliding to a stop, he dug in his toes and refused. My unfortunate cousin landed once more on his neck. Babs regained her saddle, wheeled the skewbald round and set him again at the jump, but Patch had by now decided that he'd had enough! Putting down his head in a forebodingly familiar way, he began a series of bucks. Babs, who had pulled her stirrup-leathers short for jumping, lacked the grip to keep on. She shot off to land ingloriously on the grass, while Patch cantered twenty yards and then dropped his head to graze.

'Number Four is disqualified,' the loudspeaker announced.

My heart went out to Babs as she collected Patch and made her way to join us.

'Bad luck!' I sympathised but Babs must have been choking with disappointment because she did not say anything. She just stood beside me, kicking at the grass and not even looking at the next competitors.

There were two clear rounds, followed by a straggle of unsuccessful hopefuls.

Then it was my turn to jump the course on Misty – and Babs didn't even wish me luck!

2 *Misty's clear round*

Babs' attitude was the only thing that dimmed my excitement. Surely she could have wished me luck! I would have done if our roles had been reversed. Or I *thought* I would.

I tried to put my cousin from my mind as Misty trotted on to the course. My pony's neat ears were pricked, her head was well bent, her steps springy, her hocks collectedly under her. She knew exactly what was needed. The bell went and she set off for the first fence at an eager canter. All I had to do was to take my weight off her quarters and let my hands slide forward with the reins as she extended her neck to take off.

My grey pony cleared the jump easily and set off for the next obstacle.

'That's the way, Misty!' I just touched her with my heels. 'We're racing against the clock. Not only must we get a clear round; we must do it in record time.'

All the hours that I had spent training my pony to canter this way and that, to complete figures-of-eight with change of legs and without loss of pace, came to our aid as I swung Misty sharply right-handed and gave her the freedom to increase both speed and length of stride as she neared the next fence.

Misty needed no real urging. She flew the double-oxer with space to spare. Then we were off down the hill to a stone wall with a pole on top. Jumping downhill is always difficult, and I knew it would take only the lightest brush of a hoof to dislodge that rail.

Misty seemed to sense my tension. I felt her steady herself for the jump. Then she increased her pace, taking off well in front of the obstacle and tucking up her fore-feet to make sure that she did not dislodge the pole.

Uphill again, we swung left towards the water-jump. The take-off had been churned up by the other competitors. It was easy to see that several of them had experienced trouble here.

'Steady, Misty!'

We had come at the jump carefully so as not to slip on the muddied ground but, at the same time, with enough speed to clear the width of water. Many ponies dislike jumping water, and even Misty took off so far ahead that I thought she had misjudged the spread.

I half-turned my head as we landed, expecting to hear that fateful splash which would mean that she had come down with a hind-foot in the water and lost points. But no! We were over with a foot to spare and Misty was off again, hooves drumming on the firmer turf as we approached the in-and-out, the last obstacle before we turned for home.

How were we for time?

I had no means of knowing, but I couldn't help feeling anxious as my pony steadied before jumping into the double. Was her caution losing her valuable time?

'Come on, Misty. You can do it!'

She cleared the second part of the obstacle, and I urged her to gallop faster. I was pushing her hard as we turned for the homeward stretch. She was doing so well that I badly wanted her to win. She deserved a place in the team so that she could share yet again in the competitive events she so much enjoyed.

I heeled Misty hard as we came to the most difficult obstacle of the course – a bank with post-and-rails on top and a further set of rails on the landing side. It was made like the famous Derby bank at Hickstead and was a frightening jump for a Junior Class. I think it was probably included in the course only because it would form part of the adult event later that afternoon.

Misty leapt on to the bank; then pricked her ears before twitching them back again. She was looking hard at the post-and-rails and I knew she did not like the prospect of the steep drop beyond.

As Misty hesitated I saw an exchange of glances between two Riding Club grown-ups who were standing beside the bank, scoring any faults. It was obvious that they thought my pony might refuse.

'Keep going, Misty!' I whispered. 'We'll show them!'

Taking a firm grip on my reins, I dug my heels into her sides.

Sure-footedly, Misty took the post-and-rails, pricked her ears and, tucking her hocks beneath her, slid halfway down the bank, jumped off and put in two confident strides to meet the second lot of rails that completed the jump.

'Well done, girl!' There was an involuntary gasp from one of the supervisors. I legged Misty towards the single-oxer, followed by the cut-and-laid hedge that completed the course.

'Clear round, Jackie! Good effort. You took only ten seconds longer than Copenhagen. That means you're lying third,' one of the stewards told me as I dismounted.

I could have whooped with joy. Then I remembered Babs' bitterness because her pony would never make a first-class jumper. She was leading Patch across to us

now. But instead of looking downcast she seemed strangely light-hearted.

'I've had a brainwave, Jackie – just to prove to myself that I can jump even if Patch can't. Please, please let me go round the course on Misty. I've asked one of the stewards and he says I can be fitted in later when Misty's had a breather.'

I hated myself for hesitating and then forced myself to say: 'Very well, Babs. She's all yours.'

3 *A nasty shock*

'My turn now.' Babs was excited as the last of the other competitors trotted off the course.

'And the best of luck,' I said soberly as I checked my pony's girth before my cousin mounted. 'Now don't forget. Let Misty make up her own mind when to take off.'

I don't think Babs was even listening but, in the event, it didn't matter. Right from the start, my pony jumped even better for Babs than she had done for me – probably because she already knew the course. Even the sun shining on the water-jump did not seem to put her off. She jumped it clear with a couple of feet to spare. As for the dreaded bank – well, this time Misty knew what to expect. She leaped neatly on the top, steadied herself, popped over the post-and-rails without hesitation, slid part way down, then launched herself off from the slope to fly the second lot of rails.

There was a ripple of applause from the spectators and then, with barely a second's hesitation, my pony galloped to take the single-oxer and the cut-and-laid that completed the course. Thanks to Misty, Babs had done it in record time, making her an equal first with Charles Lang – the most experienced rider of all those taking part.

'Well done, Barbara Spencer on Misty Morn. Please report to the secretary's table.'

What now? Did this mean that Babs would be picked for the team? One thing was sure. I would just scrape in, even though Misty's super performance with Babs had moved me down from third place to fourth. We couldn't both ride Misty, so perhaps the judges would find another pony who was a reliable jumper for Babs to ride.

Speculating happily, we accompanied Charles Lang and Felicity Wayne-Smith, the other two successful competitors, into the committee tent.

'Ah! Our prospective team!' Lean and horsemanlike, Colonel Graham raised his gaze from the papers on the table to look at our eager faces. 'Now, ladies first, I think.'

Shuffling the forms, he motioned me as the nearest of the three girls to the opposite chair.

'Jackie Hope,' he wrote. 'Address, please?'

'Cherry Trees Cottage, Marston.' I could hardly contain my jubilation. Here I was being signed up as an official representative of the local riding club for the National Junior Trials! I couldn't believe my luck!

'Name of pony?' the colonel prompted, 'and now your date of birth, Jackie, please.'

As I told him, a puzzled frown seemed to replace the Colonel's look of benevolence. 'So your birthday falls on the twenty-seventh of August, Jackie? That means you'll be fourteen two days before the National Championship. I wonder whether that can be allowed?' He

gestured to me to wait by the side of the table. 'We must look into the rules.'

My heart sank. I'd so counted on getting a place in the team. What now?

'Perhaps I can check for you, Colonel.' Mrs Green, the Riding Club secretary, picked up a pamphlet and took it to the daylight to study the small print.

Meanwhile Colonel Graham went on to fill in the form for Felicity Wayne-Smith. Then it was Babs' turn. Being six month's younger than I was, there was no problem over her date of birth. Babs qualified for the

Under-Fourteens without question. The only difficulty in her case came over the question of a mount.

'Now,' the Colonel said, studying Babs keenly. 'As I remember, your first round was a write-off, wasn't it?'

Babs nodded uneasily.

'That was on your own pony, Patch,' recalled the Colonel. 'Then, in contrast, on your cousin's pony, you jumped a first-class round.' He paused and tapped the table with his ball-point. 'Was that due to the pony, Babs? Or should the credit be yours? That's the question.'

Before Babs could answer, Mrs Green laid the open volume of competition-rules in front of the Colonel. Her finger pointed to the relevant paragraph.

'There's no doubt about it, I'm afraid, Colonel,' she said. 'No competitor whose fourteenth birthday falls before the date of the National Finals can compete in the Junior Classes.' She looked sympathetically across at me. 'I'm sorry, Jackie.'

'Humph!' The Colonel painstakingly studied the regulations. From over the half-moons of his reading spectacles he looked up at me. 'There's no getting round it, Jackie. It's bad luck but there it is. That leaves us with a first-class jumping pony and no rider. Now –' He gazed from me to Babs. 'The question is: Barbara Ariadne Bettina Spencer, can you be relied upon to put up as good a performance in the National Trials as you did this afternoon? More important,' he glanced back to me, 'would you, Jackie, be sufficiently self-sacrificing to let your cousin use your pony?'

I felt shattered. What could I say? How could I refuse without being absolutely selfish and mean-spirited?

'That's all right by me,' I managed to say and hoped I did not sound too unwilling.

'That's the spirit,' the Colonel said quickly, not giving me a chance to change my mind. 'Very sporting of you, m'dear.'

'Thanks, Jackie.' Babs' eyes were shining. 'I'll never be able to repay you! I'll be so careful. I won't jab Misty's mouth. I'll remember always to let her rest between rounds and I'll wisp her down when she's hot so as not to let her get a chill.'

'Well, that's settled,' said the Colonel. 'Now for the details.' He paused, as though to soften yet another blow. 'I'm going to ask rather a lot of you, Jackie. From now until the competition is over, I don't want you to ride Misty – or even to look after her. I want you to hand her over entirely to Babs. I shall be holding an intensive training course for the junior team at the Grange. We've got jumping lanes, practice fences – our own cross-country course – all the facilities, in fact.' He turned to Mrs Green. 'Who does that leave? Charles Lang? And for the time being we'll have the three runners-up as reserves so that we can see who shapes up best.'

I was so stunned by all that had happened that I barely took in the names of the reserves. Nor did I pay much attention when Mrs Green asked the Colonel about the competitors for the other classes.

'There's the new section to be considered,' she

reminded him, and dully I heard her continue; 'For the first time there's to be a competition for the Under-Eighteen team. I suppose there's no doubt who'll be selected for that?'

'No doubt at all,' confirmed the Colonel. 'We're lucky to have the Star family to take care of the entry. It's easy for the four of them to train together.'

The jumping Stars! I knew that Sally and Edmund Star were a long way below the age limit of eighteen. Evidently the twins', Dirk's and Karen's, eighteenth birthday fell after the prescribed date. There would be no question of *them* having to give up their own ponies to somebody else for weeks on end.

Six whole weeks, I thought wretchedly. For almost the whole of the summer holidays I'd be deprived of Misty.

I tried not to show my despondency as Babs chattered happily beside me on our way to collect the ponies.

'I can't ever thank you enough, Jackie. Giving up your precious Misty to me. I'd never have a chance of making the team without her, and now – why this might be the start of me having a show-jumping career.'

As we neared our ponies, Babs moved proprietorially to Misty. 'It would be best if I rode her home, wouldn't it? That's what the Colonel meant. I've got to start handling her from now on, so that she gets thoroughly used to me. She'll have to be my pony for the next six weeks, and you can ride Patch.'

'Yes, good old Patch!' I forced myself to remember

how fond I was of Babs' wayward skewbald. 'Thank you very much,' I said mechanically. Then I couldn't help blurting out what was really on my mind. I almost rounded on Babs. 'Just you be careful with Misty. I shall hold you responsible if anything happens to her. Watch it! Keep your wits about you. None of your usual scatty brainwaves! If anything happens to Misty while you are looking after her, I'll never forgive you, *never*!'

4 *I give up my pony!*

Mummy and Daddy said that I had done the right thing, but I wasn't so sure.

I couldn't help feeling piqued when I saw Babs going down to the paddock to take Misty her goodnight pieces of carrot.

'If only Babs weren't so bossy about it all, Scamp.' Bending down to press my cheek against the silky head of my golden cocker I opened my heart. 'It's bad enough to be forbidden to ride my own pony, but to have Babs say I mustn't even pat her – well, honestly, it's just . . . *impossible*!'

I didn't feel any more charitable towards my cousin, when, with what I thought to be a great deal of unnecessary performance, Babs gave Misty's already clean tack a thorough going-over before riding to the Grange next morning for the start of Colonel Graham's intensive training scheme.

While Babs, now humming happily to herself, was busy saddle-soaping the already spotless and supple leather, I wandered down to the field to bid my pony a heartfelt, if temporary, farewell. Misty would be coming back to Cherry Trees that evening but I knew that to be fair to my cousin I would have to follow Colonel

Graham's instructions and leave the care of my pony entirely to Babs.

'It won't be for long, Misty.' I put an arm across my pony's neck while she nuzzled my blazer pocket in hope of a tit-bit. 'It's only for the next six weeks, although I know it will seem long enough to you, just as it will to me.'

I took some pony nuts from my pocket and held them out on my flattened palm. Feeling the velvety touch of Misty's muzzle and the tickle of her whiskers as she lipped them up, a lump rose in my already choky throat.

'Come on, Jackie! Stop mooning!' Babs' voice from behind me made me start guiltily, though why I should feel guilty at saying 'good-bye' to my own pony goodness only knew! 'Colonel Graham said you were to leave her entirely to me.'

I gazed at Babs reproachfully. Was my own cousin and best friend really so insensitive to my feelings? Didn't she realise how hard it was for me to give up Misty even to her? Didn't she understand how disappointed I was not to be taking a place with my pony in the jumping team? Couldn't she sense my uneasy fear that something might happen to Misty when she was out of my care?

Babs must have read my thoughts because, just then, her summer-blue eyes met mine and she kicked at the grass before saying: 'I'm sorry, Jackie. Honestly I am. Don't think I don't understand, but this is my big chance. I'm grateful to you for lending me Misty. But

with your birthday falling when it does, you wouldn't have been able to compete, anyway. It's only right, really, that Misty should have a chance to show what she can do.'

Looking back, I suppose I ought to have realised that Babs was trying to be reasonable. Why did I deliberately refuse to see it? Why didn't I say something pleasant and reassuring? Instead, it seemed as though the demon of jealousy had completely taken over my tongue and before I could stop myself I retorted. 'Oh, don't be so smug!'

Then, without wishing my cousin luck, I turned and strode towards the cottage, leaving Babs too flabbergasted to say a thing. I didn't even turn my head. I couldn't. It was painful enough to hear the clip-clop of Misty's hooves as Babs rode her away.

'Cheer up, Jackie, for goodness sake,' Mummy said over lunch, 'Misty will be back to-night and meanwhile you've got Patch. Why not go for a ride this afternoon? You could go up on the Downs and take Scamp with you. He could do with a run.'

Without much enthusiasm I agreed. In spite of myself, my heart lightened as I collected the skewbald's tack and, with my cocker racing ahead, made my way to the paddock. Dear old Scamp! Mummy was right, he deserved an outing and as for Patch – well, it was hardly his fault that he wasn't Misty.

Poor Patch! He might even wonder why I was riding him. His feelings might have been hurt when he'd seen

Babs set off on Misty. Plump and lazy as he was, he was still a loyal, game pony.

On the Downs, with the wind in Patch's mane, a lark twittering high in the blue and Scamp racing ahead, I could not help but feel better.

We cantered to the hill-top beacon and I pulled up, letting my reins go slack as Patch's plump sides heaved. Scamp, too, wanted a rest. He flopped on the turf, pink tongue lolling, teeth gleaming in an exhausted doggy grin.

We weren't the only ones on the Downs that afternoon. In the distance I could see the familiar figure of Mrs Green, our riding club secretary. Auburn hair ruffled by the breeze, neatly and suitably dressed in a pale green safari suit, she was exercising her Afghans, Bazra and Mehitabel.

Seeing us, she waved, so I whistled Scamp and trotted Patch towards her to say 'hello'.

'I'm glad to see you out, Jackie.' She gave a friendly smile. 'It was hard luck having to hand over Misty and drop out of the team just because your birthday falls two days too soon.'

'Rotten!' I agreed. 'When Babs rode Misty off this morning, I felt pretty chocker, but I don't mind so much now. I feel better for having come out for a ride.'

'Anyway, I'm glad I've seen you,' said Mrs Green. 'I've had an idea . . . You may be a day or two too old for the junior team, but that would hardly disqualify you from the Under-Eighteens.'

'I'd thought of that,' I said, 'but surely the Stars are entering as a family team.'

'Yes, but they'll need a reserve,' Mrs Green pointed out, 'and from what I've heard they need someone to help exercise, too. Dirk's working for a solicitor in the town at the moment. He can't give as much time to schooling Viking as he should. Colonel Graham was talking about it only last night. The point is, Jackie, if the Stars were agreeable, would you be willing to help them out?'

My heart leapt. Would I be willing? The Stars had

already proved themselves in the junior show-jumping world. To train with them was a wonderful chance. Apart from which, the opportunity would take my mind off Misty.

'I'd love it,' I said fervently. 'But would the Stars want me?'

'Sally would, I'm sure,' said Mrs Green. 'You and she are much of an age.'

'It would be up to the older ones, though, wouldn't it?' Doubt was beginning to quench my hope. 'Dirk and Karen would have the final say.'

'Dirk, really,' Mrs Green nodded. 'It would be his horse that you'd be riding.'

My heart began to sink. 'From all I've heard, Dirk Star's a stickler. He'd have to be quite sure of my ability before he'd let me ride Viking.'

'Well, there's only one thing for it,' Mrs Green said practically. 'We must arrange for you to go over there and ride with them. Let the Stars judge your capabilities for themselves!'

5 *On trial with the Stars*

Two days later, as I trotted Patch into the stableyard at Three Paddocks, I was tensely aware that critical eyes were watching my every movement. I knew that I was on trial. What an ordeal!

Freckle-faced Sally, her tawny hair held at the nape of her neck with a slide, stood poised, one hand on a pair of reins looped from a hook, the other holding a sponge.

Fifteen-year-old Edmund looked round from brushing his piebald. Seventeen-year-old Karen, Dirk's twin, eyed me with hostility from above the bridle which she had been piecing together.

The great Dirk in person stopped in the act of picking out the hooves of a tall chestnut with one white sock and a star-like blaze. The horse was Viking, Dirk's own mount. I recognised him from the show-ring.

'Just one kind word,' I sighed to Patch. 'That's really all we need just now.'

It was Sally who guessed my feelings. 'Hello, Jackie.' She moved towards me, smiling. 'Welcome to Three Paddocks.'

'Or will it be just a case of "hail and farewell"?' Edmund sounded cynical.

'Give the girl a chance, Ed.' Dirk came to my rescue.

'It's good of you to come, Jackie. I know you understand that it's a question of deciding how you suit us and whether we'll suit you.'

'Whether she's up to riding Viking, more like.' Karen's eyes, near-violet beneath a cloud of dark hair, rested on me doubtfully. 'What's the test to be, then?' She turned to her twin. 'Are you going to put her up on the monster right away?'

'Don't listen to her, Jackie,' Sally said swiftly. 'Viking's not a monster, of course. Karen's trying to scare you. The truth is she's mad because Dirk won't hand over Viking to her.'

'That's right.' Dirk put a brotherly hand on his twin's shoulder. 'It's far better if you stick to Rowan, old girl. You and she are magic together. It would be a pity to disturb such a partnership.' He turned to me. 'I'm hoping that you, Jackie, may be able to ride Viking well enough to exercise him for me. Think you can cope?'

'I'll – I'll try.'

'Before you do that,' Edmund said bluntly, 'perhaps you'd better be quite honest as to whether you've had experience of riding a powerful horse.'

'Some,' I said shortly. Then I told them how Babs and I had helped the country-singer, Rory O'Brady, by taking charge of his two show-jumpers while he had been away on tour. [You may have read about this in my book: *Jackie and the Missing Showjumper*.] Once, too, I'd had to ride the famous Golden Boy, a Grand National winner, belonging to my ex-National-Hunt-jockey, uncle-by-marriage, Steve Rowlands. [See my book: *Jackie's Showjumping Surprise*]. 'Apart from that,' I admitted, 'I've usually ridden ponies like Misty and Patch.'

'And ridden them well, too,' said Dirk with an encouraging smile. 'From all I hear you and Misty were a sensation at the Trials the other afternoon.'

'That was Misty's doing.' I pulled Patch's reins over his head and ran up my stirrups in what I hoped was a horsemanlike way. 'Where shall I put this pony? Then we can get on with the test.'

'You sound as though you're dreading it,' summed up Karen accurately.

After unsaddling Patch and leaving him in one of the empty loose-boxes, I went over to Viking.

'Would you like me to tack him up, Dirk?'

The six-foot-high Dirk bent his dark head to look at me. 'That won't be necessary, Jackie. I'll see to him myself. I'll be riding Viking this afternoon. I want you to try Colleen.'

Karen nodded knowingly at Edmund. 'Hear that? Dirk's not trusting her with Viking until he sees how she does.'

Sally emerged from the tack-room carrying a bridle and a saddle of new-looking leather. 'I'll take you to Colleen, Jackie. Then you can put on her gear.'

Away from the others, in the hay-scented dimness of the bright bay's box, Sally warned me what to expect.

'We've not had Colleen long.' She passed the pelham bridle to me. 'She's apt to be rather unpredictable. Dirk says she's got the makings of a jumper but she's still very green.'

'Fair enough.' I led the bay mare into the yard.

Although I was full of misgivings, I was still determined not to let the Stars notice my dismay. My legs felt like jelly as I prepared to mount. I knew that I was a competent rider, but Colleen was an unknown ride. Young, skittish and still more than half-wild, she danced sideways as Dirk's shadow fell across the yard.

'Want me to give you a leg up?' he asked.

I shook my head. Somehow I had to cope on my own. Hopping after the mare as she circled, I struggled to get my leg across the saddle.

'I can manage,' I assured Dirk with a confidence I did not really feel. 'We'll be O.K.'

Dirk took his time over mounting Viking and the young mare shifted restlessly. I only hoped I was right.

6 *A dire test*

'I'll take the lead.' Dirk rode Viking towards the field gate. 'Try and keep up, but let me jump first to show you the way. We'll follow our cross-country course.'

'Good luck, Jackie!' Sally called as Colleen jiggled sideways through the gateway. 'I hope you do well. It would be lovely having you here.'

Ahead of me, Dirk approached the first fence, part of the hedge that surrounded the field. As in a real trial the obstacle was marked by flags.

'Steady, Colleen!' I tried to calm the mare as she fidgeted to be up with Viking.

The bay threw up her head trying to snatch at her bit, but I was ready for her. I shortened the curb-rein to bend her neck, at the same time driving her on with my knees.

'That's it, my beauty. Go as hard as you like now but remember that we mustn't try to overtake.'

In front of us Dirk had reached the hedge. Noticing the powerful punch that Viking gave with his quarters on take-off, I thought he might be an awkward horse to sit. Perhaps that was why Dirk had decided to try me out on Colleen before letting me ride him. Viking soared over the obstacle as though he had wings and it was easy to tell that there would not be much in the jumping field that he could not clear. From the quality of their mounts, I knew why the Stars had such a reputation among show-jumping fans.

No doubt, one day, Colleen would be as good a mount as the others. She had powerful hocks and a springy action that suggested she would have plenty of jumping power when she had been given the necessary work to muscle her up.

Letting my thoughts run on, I was unprepared for the swerve that the mare gave as she reached the jump. Instead of taking it, she swung to the left and leapt a low clump of gorse. To my shame I nearly lost my seat, but luck was with me and I just managed to push myself back into the saddle. Ahead Dirk reined up and I saw him look surprised as he turned in his saddle, wondering why I hadn't followed him.

Feeling that I had made a fool of myself, I jammed down my crash-cap. Taking a firm grip on my reins, I clapped my heels to Colleen's sides and drove her again at the brushwood spread. This time she took the jump.

'Not bad.' Dirk's reaction as we landed was guarded. 'You'll know better than to let her run out again, I dare say.'

His lips quirked before he turned his head and set Viking into a gallop.

Swinging right-handed, he made downhill for a solid-looking oxer with a ditch on the take-off side. Viking cleared it easily and Dirk turned him in a circle and reined up to see how Colleen and I would fare. At that moment slanting rain drove towards us in a sudden squall. Colleen flattened her ears and tucked in her tail. As we reached the fence her neck stiffened and I knew that she intended to refuse.

On the other side of the jump Dirk was waiting, eyebrows raised. I could sense his disappointment as he thought that I was going to have another failure. He must think that it had hardly been worth his time to bring me out for a test ride.

Well, I'd show him!

I drove my heels into the mare's reluctant sides. 'Run out again, would you?' I said grimly, 'well, you've got to learn some time and it had better be now!'

I gave her a whack with my switch.

Colleen shot into the air, clearing the ditch and oxer with a leap that would have done credit to a Grand National entry.

'Well done,' Dirk applauded as we sailed over to join him.

Finding herself well over the jump, Colleen jingled her bit, tossing her head and dancing sideways as if eager to repeat the performance.

'Hold hard!' cautioned Dirk. 'The next obstacle is a gate. I want you to go first and open it.'

The ground flattened out, and Colleen charged forward, thinking the gate was an obstacle to be jumped. Instead she would have to pull up so that I could open it.

I found myself unable to stop the mare.

Standing well back, she launched herself at the gate.

There was a hollow on the landing side and the ground looked a long way below. Beneath me Colleen seemed to take a sudden nose-dive. I was left behind for less than a second but when the mare landed I could not stop myself pitching right over her head to land on my feet on the ground.

'At least you remembered to hang on to her reins,' Dirk said drily as he expertly manoeuvred Viking through the gate to join us. 'O.K., Jackie. Get back into the saddle. I've seen all I need.'

'I'm afraid I'm not good enough for you.' Downcast, I fiddled with my reins.

'On the contrary,' Dirk said with a half-smile. 'You're not bad. At least you've got guts. Like Colleen you need more schooling, but by the time you've joined in our work-outs and ridden Viking for a few weeks, you might be good enough to be our reserve.'

The rain stopped as suddenly as it had begun. Now the sun shone, highlighting the strand of dark hair that fell from Dirk's cap.

We rode back beside the river. Presently we saw a group of horses grazing in the water meadow. There were five of them – a couple of leggy youngsters, one chestnut and one black, a three-year old bay and a flea-bitten grey mare with a perky Palomino foal. Colleen shrilly called to them. She began to dance about, and it took all my attention to prevent her flying the fence to join the group.

'Those were our young stock,' Dirk explained when we were past. 'In the jumping world you have to look ahead. We'll make the name of Star really famous one day, given the right luck.'

'You're famous already,' I enthused. 'There isn't a pony boy or girl in this whole county who won't envy me my chance, once they know I've got the good luck to train with the Stars!'

'Local fame – that's one thing.' Dirk's mouth twitched with amusement. 'It's the big time we're really after. That's what my twin, Karen, says. At the moment I am filling in time doing clerical work for a Marston solicitor before going on to University, but Karen's not keen for me to take up law as a profession. She's even more ambitious than I am, and a hard task mistress. She won't allow slacking from any member of the team. You'll be working with her mostly, Jackie, so you'll need to be on your toes.'

Dirk's words filled me with misgiving. He had been comparatively easy to satisfy. But what would his twin say when she knew he'd given me the job?

How long would my luck hold?

7 *We quarrel*

That evening, although Babs chattered on as usual about riding Misty, I barely listened. I had so much to think about – my meeting with the Stars; the test-ride on Colleen and, above all, Dirk's approval.

'You're not listening, Jackie.' At last Babs' voice penetrated my thoughts. 'Colonel Graham wants to try Misty in a standing martingale.'

'A standing martingale! Why?' The implication of what Babs was saying alerted me with a jerk. 'If Colonel Graham wants Misty to have a standing martingale, it can be for only one reason – to stop her throwing her head up when you jab her mouth.' All my pent-up resentment that Babs should be riding my pony came out explosively. 'You'll ruin her as a jumper. You've always been heavy-handed. I ought to have known better than to agree to let you ride my pony.'

'If you think that, I'm not going to sit here drinking cocoa with you while you make insinuations.' Impetuously, Babs pushed back her chair and in so doing happened to brush against Scamp, waking him to reality from his rabbit-filled dreams on the hearth-rug. 'You're jealous, Jackie. That's what's wrong with you.'

'Jealous, am I? Why should I be jealous of you, when

the Stars have picked me for their reserve for the Under-Eighteens? That's a step up from the juniors, and no mistake.'

'Oh, you're impossible!' In her annoyance, Babs stumbled on Scamp's paw, sending him yelping out of her way.

'Look where you're putting your feet, you clumsy idiot,' I scolded Babs. 'Come here, Scamp, and let me rub it better.'

Babs must have had the same idea because, at the moment I reached for my spaniel's paw, my cousin bent on a similar mission. With a crack our heads struck.

'You lunatic!' Babs clutched at her head. 'You might have fractured my skull.'

'No chance. Your head's far too thick,' I scoffed. 'You're such a dim-wit that you're a positive menace. No animal sense whatever! That's what's wrong with you. First you're in such danger of spoiling Misty's mouth that Colonel Graham wants to put her in a standing martingale. Now you almost maim Scamp.'

Just then the door opened and Mummy looked in. 'What's wrong, you two?' She glanced from Babs' flushed face to mine. 'Don't say you've been quarrelling? I know what it is. You're both over-tired and fractious. Better get an early night, the pair of you. You'll feel better tomorrow.'

Without another word Babs left the sitting-room and went upstairs. Not wanting to have to talk to her again that evening, I hurried out of the house. I told Mummy that I needed to put Patch's tack ready for the morning.

Instead I went down to the ponies. Misty and Patch were both grazing. Not wanting Babs to hear me I whistled softly.

Patch's brown-and-white head lifted immediately. He came trotting to the gate, hopeful for tit-bits. Misty, however, just went on grazing. It was as though she could not be bothered to come to my call. It seemed to me then as if the few days that Babs had been riding Misty had severed the bond of years between me and my pony.

Forgetful of Babs, I whistled again, then called: 'Come on, Misty, you silly pony! Don't you want some carrot?' My voice must have carried further than I intended. Next minute the bedroom window opened and Babs' head thrust out.

'Leave Misty alone, Jackie! Too many tit-bits are bad for her,' she called bossily. 'Besides you're not supposed to interfere. Colonel Graham said nothing should be allowed to break the *rapport* between rider and pony.'

Seething, I whistled to Scamp and went into the house. Making a great performance of cleaning my jodhpur boots, I postponed going upstairs. When I reached the bedroom Babs was pretending to be asleep. She must have been just as determined as I was not to have any further conversation.

Next morning, when I awoke, she was already downstairs.

Well, if that was the way Babs wanted it, I didn't care, I told myself as I went into the bathroom to brush my teeth.

It was half-past seven and I knew that I'd have plenty of time to ride over to the Stars for nine o'clock – the hour Karen had scheduled for the start of the day's schooling.

Three Paddocks was not much more than a mile away. It shouldn't take me long to get there, even on Patch. I waited until I saw Babs leave the cottage and cross the orchard with Misty's bridle before I went downstairs. By the time I had eaten breakfast my cousin had left.

Ten minutes later I was in the tack room collecting Patch's gear. I'd folded the girth over the saddle before I realised anything was wrong. Then I noticed that one of the stirrups was missing. The leather lay unbuckled on the bench but the iron had gone! Where could it be? Surely Babs hadn't been so spiteful as to tamper with Patch's tack? She knew I would have a tight schedule. Didn't she realise how important it was for me to arrive in good time on my first day with the Stars?

She *must* have done it on purpose! How could she be so mean?

Frantically I hunted for the missing stirrup iron. I looked on the shelves, under the bench, even in the first aid box.

It wasn't until almost ten minutes later that I noticed a folded piece of paper beneath the unbuckled stirrup-leather. Was this Babs' idea of a joke?

Angrily I unfolded the note.

Dear Jackie,

This leather hasn't been properly cleaned – my cousin had

scrawled. *To teach you to take more care of other people's tack, I've removed the iron. You'll find it under the saddle-soap tin, just to rub the message in!*

Cheerio!

Babs.

Furious, I snatched up the tin of saddle soap, retrieved the stirrup iron and threaded the leather through. True, in the hasty wipe over that I'd given Patch's equipment the previous evening, I'd overlooked a streak of dried sweat on the inside of the leather. Just the same, Babs had no right to delay me. Of all the priggish behaviour! As if she'd never been guilty of skimping tack-cleaning!

Now I'd be late. Karen Star would be able to report to her twin, Dirk, that I couldn't even be relied on to arrive at the agreed time!

Seething, I went to catch Patch.

8 *I'm blamed*

I was well and truly late.

The clock on the Parish church tower struck the half-hour as I turned into the Stars' lane. Karen would be livid!

Not only Karen was upset, it seemed: Sally's freckled face was strained as she met me at the gate.

'For heaven's sake, Jackie, what's kept you? You'll have made Dirk late. He asked permission not to get to the office until ten o'clock this morning so that he could see you start off with Viking.' She grasped Patch's reins. 'Here! I'll see to the pony. Hurry into the yard and, for Pete's sake, put your cap straight. You look as if you've been thrown into a gorse bush – and you know what a stickler Karen is!'

The Star twins were waiting for me outside the loose box. Edmund was hovering near to witness my humiliation.

'This is the limit!' Karen exclaimed before I had a chance to explain. 'At least you might have the good manners to get here on time. Dirk's been waiting for over half-an-hour. Now he'll be late for work.'

'Oh, Dirk, I'm so sorry,' I said, appalled.

'Well, don't let's waste any more time.' Dirk led out

his chestnut show-jumper. 'Now that you are here, I want to see how Viking goes for you.'

I'd come prepared with a pocketful of apple peelings. Before mounting I offered a piece to the chestnut. After eating it, Viking lifted his nose and wrinkled back his lips showing his gums. It was as though he were grinning at me. Had we come to an understanding?

'Oh, get on with it, Jackie,' Karen said impatiently. 'Don't tell me you're too scared to start!'

Hoping that I had won the big horse's trust, I tried not to let Karen rattle me. Deliberately I bent my head under the saddle-flap to check the girths.

'Oh, for goodness' sake!' Karen groaned.

I bit back any retort as I ran the stirrup irons down the leathers and tested them against my outstretched arm for length.

'Fair enough, Jackie,' Dirk said, and Karen looked daggers. 'Always check a horse's tack especially if you're going to jump.'

Just then Sally had come back from unsaddling Patch and joined Edmund and the others to watch me mount. Then, with Sally leading the way, we went into the jumping paddock where there were varied obstacles, some of them large and solid-looking. To my relief Dirk disregarded the formally laid-out course, indicating instead an exercise 'grid' at the side.

First there were three poles lying on the ground, a horse's stride apart. Next came six oil drums lying on their sides. A further stride away two upended oil drums and a pole made the final jump.

'I want you to trot over the poles and then take the jumps, Jackie,' Dirk instructed.

'Do you mind if I canter round the field first?' I suggested. 'I'd like to get used to Viking's action.'

'Very well,' Dirk nodded. 'But don't take too long.'

'I'd have thought Jackie had wasted enough time already,' Karen put in. 'All the same, I suppose we must be fair.'

Viking's stride seemed long compared with Patch's or Misty's. At the start of each came that powerful punch with his quarters that I had noticed when I had seen him jump. There was no doubt that over big fences Viking would be a difficult horse to sit.

The 'grid' exercise wasn't much of a problem, however. As Dirk had said the horse was used to this routine. I, too, had done similar exercises with Misty at home. All the same, at first I found Viking's impulsion unnerving, even over such small jumps as these, but Dirk sent us round a couple more times and, by then, I had become more accustomed to the chestnut's punch.

'You'll do, Jackie,' Dirk nodded when I finally reined up. 'I must go now or the partners will give me a black mark. I'll hand you over to Karen.'

The other three Stars mounted and joined me and soon we were working hard, doing suppling exercises, trotting and cantering circles and figures-of-eight and then jumping. At first we jumped singly, then as a team.

The day passed quickly and soon I realised that I was

learning more than I could ever have hoped to do on my own. Like Babs I was getting the chance really to make something of my jumping.

During the afternoon we rode over the Stars' own cross-country course. Viking needed some controlling as the excitement of jumping with the others gripped him. The pace was hot; some of the jumps were alarming. Several times I nearly lost my seat, but fate and Viking were with me and I managed to stick on.

Karen hadn't the grace to say anything pleasant. 'Unsaddle now and rub Viking down,' she instructed. 'He's apt to break out in a sweat from excitement so we use a 'string vest'. Slip it on him before you get his water. Then put down his bedding before you give his feed.'

I'd just buckled on Viking's anti-sweat rug, the coarse, nylon-mesh 'string vest' to which Karen had referred, when I heard a familiar whinny. Misty! What was she doing here? Her whinny was followed by a clatter of pony hooves.

'Jackie! Are you there?' Babs called out.

'What do you want?' I turned from Viking coldly to regard my cousin.

'To apologise, Jackie.' By now Babs had dismounted from Misty and was standing fiddling with the bolt of the next door loose-box. 'I wanted to say I was sorry, Jackie. I shouldn't have hidden that stirrup-iron this morning. Did it take you long to find it? Were you late?'

'Of course I was late,' I said shortly, 'and keep away from that loose-box door.'

The annoyance in my voice seemed to make Babs nervous. She looked as flustered as I had felt under Karen's needling that morning. Now I was getting my own back!

'I'm sorry, Jackie,' Babs said uncomfortably. 'I really am. We can't let things go on like this between us.

We're not just cousins. We've always been friends.' Her fingers tightened on the bolt of Colleen's box.

Unsure of strangers in her new surroundings, the bay's head snaked out dangerously.

Involuntarily, Babs stepped back, pulling the door with her. In a flash Colleen was out. Before either of us could grab her, the bay charged between us, sending us both to the ground. From the next loose-box, Sally dashed to try to grab the mare's head-collar. Colleen snorted, curtseyed away, and stamped both forefeet at Edmund who had come running from the tack-room to jump for her head. Alarmed, Edmund backed out of the way and Colleen headed for the field-gate while Karen ran out of the feed-store.

'That's done it!' exclaimed Dirk's twin. 'The mare's running riot. I might have known, Jackie, that your coming here meant trouble!'

9 *Something dreadful*

As the runaway mare cleared the gate into the paddock, Karen ran to Rowan's loose-box.

'Grab your ponies and follow,' she called over her shoulder.

I snatched Misty's reins from my cousin and swung myself into the saddle.

'Get Patch,' I yelled at Babs as I cantered across the yard and flung open the gate. 'He's in the far loose-box.'

Colleen was by now prancing across the paddock, head and tail up, neighing shrilly. Leaving the gate open for the three Stars to follow, I put Misty after her at a gallop.

The mare seemed to be heading for the Downs and I knew that if we did not catch her quickly the chase might take hours. Karen bucketed past me on Rowan, racing for the top of the field to try to head off Colleen. Sally and Edmund thudded behind.

Colleen whinnied again, and this time her call was answered by one of the youngsters from the river-field. Shrilling a reply she swung downhill. Her hooves barely seemed to touch the turf as she sped to the bottom and flew the cut-and-laid hedge into the next meadow.

Turning Misty I swung after her. I reached the hedge ahead of the others and put my pony at the jump.

Misty soared over. With barely a check she galloped after Colleen. Behind us Karen and Rowan were catching up. Although only fourteen-two hands high, Misty was fast. Fleet of foot and with my light weight in the saddle, she made a spanking show of speed. We were neck and neck with Karen as we took the hedge.

Ahead of us Colleen jumped the fence into the river-field. Then she was amok with the youngsters, rearing and pawing the air in her excitement, plunging and lashing her heels at the nearest.

'The foal!' Karen gasped, pointing ahead to where the young palomino's lint-white mane gleamed in the sunlight as he cantered round the squealing horses.

I gave Misty a whack with my reins. Although my pony was doing her best, it was not enough. Somehow we must get to the runaway before the foal got hurt.

As I rode Misty at the fence into the water-meadow, Karen drove Rowan across our path.

'Get back, you idiot!' she flung at me. 'Let me tackle this.'

Misty's hocks slid beneath her and she pulled up short.

'Karen's right, Jackie.' Edmund halted piebald Brigand beside me. 'There are enough frightened animals in the meadow without any more. The best way we can help is on foot.'

Sally joined us as we looped our mounts' reins through the fence and clambered over. Somehow

Karen, on Rowan, had managed to cut Colleen out from the other horses. Riding Rowan up to the run-away, Karen leaned forward to grab at the bay's head-collar.

The mare was too quick for her. Tossing her head she bobbed away, turned on her hocks, and pranced back to the herd. She was making straight for Sally and me.

'Stop her, you two!' Karen ordered. 'The foal might get killed. Stand your ground. Catch her somehow!'

Beside me the colour drained from Sally's face. My knees were shaking, but I knew we must not give way. Suddenly Edmund ran between us. He hurled himself at the mare, managed to grasp her head-collar and clung on.

Squealing, Colleen threw up her head. She reared, trying to jerk free. Before Sally and I could reach her, she brought her forefeet down, trampling Edmund on to the turf. Then, shocked at what she had done, she stood trembling while Sally and I caught at her mane. Sally transferred her grip to the mare's head-collar while I just stood shock-still. Colleen's mane was in my grasp as I gazed, horrified, at Edmund lying motionless on the grass.

Karen slid from Rowan's back to bend over her brother. Colleen's hoof marks showed muddily on the front of his shirt. Karen pulled off her jacket and, folding it into a pad, edged it under Edmund's head. As she did so she looked towards Colleen and then to me.

'Don't just stand there gaping, Jackie. This may be all your fault but at least you can try to make yourself useful. Ride to the house and get help! Hurry!'

There was no sign of Babs when I galloped Misty back to Three Paddocks to break the news of Edmund's accident to Mrs Star.

I supposed that by the time my cousin had saddled Patch she had seen that the rest of us were about to catch up with the runaway. Then, feeling guilty at having been responsible for letting out Colleen, she had ridden off before anyone could blame her for the incident. She could not have seen what had happened to Edmund or she would have hurried to help.

I panted out the news of the mishap to Edmund's mother, Mrs Star, and she reached for the telephone. She alerted the doctor, her husband and Dirk. Then she set off across the fields to be with Edmund, leaving me to await the doctor's arrival.

I couldn't help blaming myself. If I hadn't quarrelled with Babs, she wouldn't have come to Three Paddocks to apologise and, in her distress, been so agitated as to fiddle with the bolt of the loose-box and let Colleen out. The mare would not have bolted and run amok among the young stock, and Edmund would not have been hurt in trying to save the foal. If only I hadn't been so impatient with my cousin!

To take my mind off my anxieties, I busied myself with the routine of evening stables – cleaning out the loose-boxes, putting down fresh straw and filling water buckets ready for when Karen and Sally would return with Colleen, Brigand and their own mounts.

Dirk and his father dead-heated with the doctor in arriving at Three Paddocks; so there was no need for me to guide anyone to the scene of the accident. With Dirk leading the way and the ambulance men carrying a stretcher, they hurried to the river field.

Nobody seemed to take any notice of me, and I did not know whether to go with them or to stay behind at Three Paddocks. I decided to carry on with the stable jobs. Even so, it seemed a long time before they all returned, the doctor walking beside the stretcher with Mr and Mrs Star, while Dirk, Karen and Sally followed with the horses.

Karen looked at me with icy indifference and Dirk was too preoccupied to notice me. I felt invisible.

'What did the doctor say?' I summoned up my

courage to ask Sally. 'Is Edmund badly hurt?'

'Two cracked ribs and severe concussion at least,' the youngest Star said unhappily. 'He won't be riding again for weeks.'

I tried to say something but I was too upset. Helplessly I was aware that Dirk and Karen were leading in the four horses.

Then I managed to say in a small voice, 'I've put down the bedding and the water buckets and the hay-nets. Is there anything else I can do?'

'Yes, Jackie.' Dirk didn't even turn to me as he fastened Brigand's door. 'Please go home.' Then, because I suppose he noticed me looking tearful, he added: 'your mother'll be worried if you're late.'

10 *Jackie is jealous*

When I went into the cottage I was flabbergasted to see Babs' suitcase standing in the hall. The label on the suitcase read: Miss B. A. B. Spencer, care of Colonel and Mrs Graham, The Grange, Marston!

Before I could recover, Mummy and Babs came out of the sitting room.

'Thank goodness, you're back, dear.' My mother gave a tight smile. 'It's just as well that you haven't unsaddled Misty because now Babs can get off right away. I've telephoned the Grahams and they're expecting her for supper. Daddy and I will take her suitcase there when we've had our own meal.'

'Just what's going on?' My puzzled gaze moved from my cousin to my mother. 'Surely you're not going to let Babs take Misty with her to stay at the Grahams.'

'We thought it was best, dear,' my mother said quietly. 'With the Trials coming up and you two continually squabbling it might be better for you to be apart for a while.'

Babs eyes evaded mine. 'I'm sorry, Jackie. It's just that I don't seem to be able to do *anything* right. I rode over to Three Paddocks to apologise and that just brought disaster!'

'Yes. Edmund's in hospital. His mother's upset and Karen's saying Colleen's not to be trusted. Goodness knows what'll become of her.' I couldn't stop myself blaming Babs. 'She might be shot or – even worse – sold without a warranty and you know what that means . . . all because of you fiddling with that bolt and letting her out. You're not fit to be trusted with horses.' I looked from Babs to my mother. 'Goodness knows what you were thinking of, Mummy, saying she could take Misty.'

'Oh, Jackie, don't!' Babs was near to tears. 'We used to be such friends. We had wonderful times together and now everything's ruined. I wish I'd never been given a place in the Riding Club team. Then things might have gone on just as they were. Neither of us would ever have become show-jumpers but at least you wouldn't have grown to hate me as you do now.'

With a cold glance at me, Mummy gave Babs' shoulder a consoling pat. 'Try not to worry about it, dear. Give your mind to your jumping and do your best to enjoy life.' She kissed my cousin's cheek. 'Jackie will come to her senses in time. Off you go now, Babs! Make sure Misty settles in comfortably at the Grange. Your uncle and I will bring over your case after supper.'

'Goodbye, Jackie.' Babs' voice was an apologetic whisper as she passed me in the hall.

I felt too devastated to reply. I just gazed at Mummy's blurred face. I knew I'd behaved badly but Mummy's show of affection for Babs and rejection of me really hurt. Mummy had sounded so cross, not at all like my usually kind and sympathetic mother. In fact she seemed more like an exasperated schoolmistress, impatient with a wayward pupil.

Very upset, I must have looked at her as though she were a stranger because suddenly she became Mummy again.

'I love you dearly, Jackie, but I just can't ignore Babs' point of view.'

I tilted my chin.

'Fair enough, Mummy,' I forced myself to say. 'But I wouldn't be human if I didn't hate Babs taking over my pony.'

Mummy put her arm around my shoulders.

'At least you've been given the chance to ride with the Stars, Jackie,' she consoled. 'That should be enough for any girl.'

'Ride with the Stars!' I groaned. 'After today's disaster they're not likely to want me.'

So it was with a feeling of dread that I reported at Three Paddocks the next morning.

'You've turned up, have you?' Karen looked up from handing her twin's briefcase into the Mini. 'I'm not sure there's any point in your coming. With Edmund out of the team we can't hope to compete. You may as well go back home.'

'Jackie go home? Nonsense!' Dirk opened the door of his car and got out to face his sister. 'There's no reason why Jackie shouldn't take Edmund's place in the team,

Karen. She'll need to get used to Brigand, of course, and I shall still want her to put in some time on Viking to keep him in trim for me.' His brown eyes met mine quizzically. 'Rather a tall order, Jackie. Do you think you can cope?'

A second chance!

'I'll do my best,' I vowed. 'Really I will.'

Brigand handled easily. At just fifteen hands he was nearer to Misty's size than the sixteen-hand Viking. Karen, Sally and I cantered to warm up. Then we rode serpentines. The piebald was well-balanced and had an excellent mouth. Edmund was a good rider and there was no doubt that his horse had been well-schooled.

We put the horses over the 'grid' and then tackled practice jumps. Brigand jumped easily and well and I found that, in spite of all that had happened, I began to feel more hopeful.

After a while we set out to ride the cross-country course. Brigand was on his toes but I managed to collect him and keep his weight on his hocks. Used to jumping with Sally's and Karen's mounts as part of a team he readily kept his place.

We cleared the last of the hedges and came to the water-jump. The going was muddy and I was so occupied with picking the best spot for Brigand to take off that I did not immediately notice the lean figure and weather-beaten face of a youth who stood watching us from the side of the jump.

The piebald saw him and swerved. His feet slid almost from under him. Using my heels and my calves I tried to collect him but he was into the water before he recovered.

Sally, on Woodbine, was hard on his heels. Brigand and Woodbine took off too close to each other and both landed short to splash into the water. Brigand slipped again and, in spite of my efforts to keep his head up, he stumbled and almost came down.

In a flash the youth who had been leaning against the fence ran to my aid.

'Easy there, my beauty.' Speaking in a soft Irish accent he took hold of Brigand's bridle to steady him and help him out of the water. 'Yes, easy does it. There's the fine horse!'

Ahead, Karen reined up Rowan and wheeled.

'And just who may you be?' She regarded the youth closely. 'What are you doing on our land?'

'I'm Barney O'Rorke.' A slow smile lit up his handsome face. 'I've come from Colonel Graham's to offer my services, hearing that you were short-handed, having had an accident with a wild horse.'

Although his tone was deferential, I noticed a look of almost mocking amusement in his eyes, though Karen seemed unaware of it.

'Accident?' she echoed. 'Where did you hear this tittle-tattle?'

'The young lady who told me was worried for you all – and for the mare,' said Barney O'Rorke.

'Very kind of her, I'm sure!' Karen's eyes were still on Barney. 'Was this young lady's name Barbara Spencer?'

'Babs, herself,' declared Barney.

Karen gave me a hard stare. 'I wish your cousin would mind her own business, Jackie.'

'She was only in a worry for the mare, miss.' Now there was a touch of wheedling in Barney's tone. 'Same as I'm sure that you are, Miss. Babs said you might be thinking of selling her or else of having her shot.

T'would be a pity for that to happen. So here I am. I'm used to wild horses. We breed them in Ireland an' I understand your wild mare is Irish.'

'So you're a horseman?' Now Karen's gaze swept over the youth. 'How old are you?'

'Eighteen in October.'

'I see.' Karen's eyes swivelled to me and then her tone to Barney suddenly changed. 'Well, if you can ride as well as most of your countrymen we may be able to make use of you, Barney. Come along.' She nudged Rowan to walk on. 'We'll go back to the stables and introduce you to Colleen. After lunch you can try out Viking. Oh, and we'll see how you ride Brigand. Then Jackie will have no need to ride any of our horses. She can use the time to make herself really useful. She can clean the tack and muck out instead.'

11 Barney's way with horses

I was determined to do the menial jobs with a pretence of cheerfulness. I did not want to be ordered off the scene. Besides I was curious to see just how good Barney might be with horses.

'Is this the wicked mare, then?' The Irish youth slid back the bolt of Colleen's box and entered. The mare shifted her feet, laid back her ears and rolled her eyes in his direction. 'Sure and you're a beautiful horse for all the fright you've had.'

Barney placed a hand on the bay's quarters, then slid it to her withers, ready to loose the slip knot and free her head.

Colleen's ears were still back. She watched the Irish youth warily.

'You're wondering who I might be now, aren't you?'

To our astonishment Barney bent his head and blew softly at the mare. It was almost as if he were a horse himself and he was using their own method of greeting. The mare's ears swivelled forward. Then she blew back at him!

'There! Now you know me!' Barney untied her head and began to gentle her, making crooning noises as he fondled her muzzle while Karen, Sally and I watched, amazed.

'That's more than she's let any of us do since she came,' Sally said admiringly. 'You've certainly got a magic touch with horses, Barney.'

Barney O'Rorke's eyes flashed a dancing gleam. 'The Irish understand each other,' he laughed. 'Take this mare – there she was, put into a horse-box and jolted off from the dear green fields of Ireland. Chivvied up the gangway into the hold of a ship; then loaded up, brought here and put into a loose-box with never a friendly voice. Can you wonder at it that she's wild? Give me a few days with her and I'll have her settled in. It would be better if none of you tried to ride her until she feels more at home.'

'Dirk's ridden her already,' Sally told him, 'and so has Jackie.'

'Just the once,' I explained. 'It was when Dirk was trying to decide whether to let me ride Viking.'

'If you passed that test, there's surely nothing wrong with your horsemanship, Jackie,' Barney said. 'To ride a green mare like this one takes guts and understanding – and good hands, too.'

Just then Karen came on the scene. 'Let's get on with it.' Impatiently she tapped her switch against her leg as she turned to Barney. 'I want to see you ride Brigand. If you can jump as well as you can charm horses, you can replace Edmund in our team.'

'I thought Jackie was going to take Edmund's place.' Sally's hazel eyes met mine in sympathy.

'Don't worry,' I said with a sigh. 'With a horseman like Barney, you won't need me.'

Barney was an instinctive rider. He jumped as if he and his mount were one. If he felt the least misgiving at the sight of the most awkward fence or the steepest drop, he did not show it. Brigand respected him. The horse seemed to go even better for him than he had done for Edmund and – oh, dear – it was only too obvious that there was no need for me in the Stars' team.

When Dirk returned from the office that evening Karen coaxed Barney to put on a special display for him.

'Sorry to rub it in, Jackie.' She turned to me with an over-sweet smile as Barney put the piebald over the wide spread of the triple bar in a way that made the difficult jump look easy. 'But I wanted Dirk to see for himself that Barney's jumping is ahead of yours – or even Edmund's. Sorry, Jackie, but you're out.'

'I know that.' I tried hard not to sound too dismayed. 'You won't need me any more.' I felt Dirk's hand on my arm and I was determined to make things easier for him. 'It's been wonderful while it lasted and I've learnt a lot from you all.' I turned away, not wanting them to see that I was nearly in tears. 'Good luck, everybody.'

'Just a minute, Jackie.' Dirk's tone was friendly, 'there's still room for you here –'

'Here we go again,' groaned Karen. 'You must be out of your horsy mind, Dirk.'

'Dry up, Karen.' Dirk turned to meet my gaze with a protective smile. 'I want Barney to concentrate on Brigand, Jackie, but you'll still be needed to exercise Viking while I'm away at the office.'

I would have been in heaven if I hadn't realised that Karen still wouldn't want me at the Stars' – that she would go on being unpleasant and would find fault with everything I did.

I felt the need to confide in somebody. If only Babs were still my friend!

'Oh, don't look so soulful, Scamp!' I scolded my spaniel that evening as he sat at the gate, waiting hopefully for a walk while I turned Patch into the Cherry Trees paddock. 'The whole world doesn't revolve round you, you know!'

Scamp's answer was to fetch his lead.

'Oh, very well,' I said impatiently. 'I suppose I'd better take you for a run.'

Just then the telephone rang and I ran into the house.

'Babs here,' a small voice said at the other end of the line

'Telepathy!' I exclaimed.

'Why?' Was my cousin's tone hopeful? 'Were you just about to telephone me, Jackie?'

'Well, I was thinking about you,' I said.

'That's something, I suppose.' Babs seemed encouraged to go on. 'It's like this, Jackie. I've been wondering whether I did the right thing in sending Barney O'Rorke to Three Paddocks. Colonel Graham didn't seem to want him here, but I could see he was wizard with horses. I thought he might be able to charm Colleen so that the Stars wouldn't get rid of her. I

couldn't bear to think of her being shot or sold.'

I warmed. This was the soft-hearted Babs who'd shared all my pony years.

'Nor could I,' I agreed. In my mind's eye I saw the problem mare's bay face, her velvet muzzle and the liquid eyes that were kindly when they weren't wild with alarm.

'Then I did the right thing?' Babs' voice was now eager. 'Barney's getting on well there is he?'

'Too well!' I tried not to sound bitter. 'The Stars have given him Edmund's place in the team.'

'The place you should have had!' Babs groaned. 'Oh, Jackie! I am so sorry. I only wanted to help.'

'You did help.' I knew my cousin had genuinely tried to do her best. 'It doesn't matter, Babs. It doesn't *really*, and Barney's been wonderful with Colleen. That's the important thing. Even Karen thinks the mare may turn out well after all. As for the Trials, well the Stars will stand a much better chance with Barney in the team. He jumps better than I do. He's a born show-jumper. If he gave his mind to it he might even reach Olympic standard. And – talking of jumping –' I couldn't help being inquisitive – 'how's Misty getting on?'

'Fine.' Then Babs must have realised she was stretching the truth to tell me what I wanted to hear. 'At least, she was doing well – until yesterday. Then she started to knock everything down. Colonel Graham thinks she may be getting stale. We haven't jumped her today. She's having a rest.'

'A rest? Not jumping well?' My voice was shrill with

anxiety. 'That's not like my Misty! Are you sure she's not sickening for something?'

'Well, she's eating well,' reported Babs, 'and her coat's fine. Colonel Graham took her temperature and it was normal.' My cousin's voice tailed off. Then she said slowly: 'I think she may be pining for you, Jackie. Perhaps it would be a good thing for you to come over tomorrow.' She paused. Then she said with a rush: 'Both Misty and I've been so miserable without you, Jackie. Can't we go back to being *real* friends? I won't ride Misty in the Trials if you don't want me to. I've improved so much now that I'm sure Colonel Graham could find me another mount.'

'Don't be such a chump, Babs,' I told my cousin fondly. 'Of course you must ride Misty. You'll have a much better chance on her than you would on any other pony.'

'Jackie!' My mother's voice rose above the television noise from the sitting-room. 'It's getting late. Time you were going to bed. I'll take Scamp for his walk.'

'Coming, Mummy!' I called. Then I said into the mouthpiece: 'You heard that, Babs? I've got to go. I'll be at the Grange tomorrow afternoon to see both you and Misty.'

My heart felt lighter as I went upstairs. I knew that I would sleep more soundly that night than I had done for ages. Edmund Star was making good progress in the hospital; Barney had brought about Colleen's reprieve and – as for Babs – she and I were again going to be best friends as well as cousins, just as we'd always been. I knew after all that I wanted Babs to ride Misty in the Trials and I wanted them both to do well.

Perhaps I was no longer jealous.

12 Reunion – through Misty!

Misty was standing in a corner of the home-field when I arrived at the Grange next afternoon. Her head was low and she was resting a hind foot. She looked miserable. She was ill, I decided impulsively.

Jumping down from Patch and leaving the reins trailing, I ran the last few yards of the drive.

'Misty!' I called. 'Misty!' I climbed over the rails to run to my beloved pony.

Patch paused before cropping the verge and added his voice to mine, neighing a greeting to his former companion.

Misty seemed to listen. Her head came up and she twitched back an ear. Next moment, with a whinny of recognition, she was cantering towards me. So she wasn't ill!

'Misty!' I exclaimed, overjoyed. 'There's nothing wrong with you. It's just that you've been missing me and your own home.'

Thankfully my arms went around my pony's neck and I buried my face in her mane. So engrossed was I in the reunion that I was barely conscious that Babs had burst out of the tack-room and raced towards Patch who was now enjoying a similar fuss.

Babs and I became aware of each other's presence. Still patting our respective ponies we looked round. Our gazes met, and we each gave a sheepish smile.

'Thank goodness Misty seems to be all right,' I said.

'I told you she was just fretting.' Babs was almost her usual perky self. 'I must admit I've been pining for Patch too.'

Just then Colonel Graham's Range Rover swept up the drive. Drawing level with us the Colonel applied his brakes, opened the door, and got out.

'It's good to see you, Jackie,' he said warmly. His glance swept over Misty. 'The grey looks a different animal since you appeared. Seems I was wrong, after all. Perhaps she wasn't stale. Perhaps she was just missing her owner.'

'It's my fault, Colonel Graham,' said Babs. 'I shouldn't have brought her to stay here. With not going back to Cherry Trees at night she must have thought she'd been given away.'

'And you haven't, my beauty.' My fingers strayed lovingly through my pony's mane. I patted her neck. 'You're still my pony, Misty, now and for always. When the Trials are all over you'll be coming back home.'

Colonel Graham looked at us consideringly. 'I think she'd better go back to Cherry Trees before then.' He looked from me to Babs and back again. 'I can see you two have made up your differences, so why don't we go back to square one? Babs and Misty could sleep at Cherry Trees and ride over each morning to practise with the team. How's that?'

Babs' gaze turned on me enquiringly. 'What do you say, Jackie?'

'Super!' I agreed quickly. 'There's nothing I'd like more.'

'Well, Misty's quite used to Babs now,' said Colonel Graham. 'So why don't you ride her for a change, Jackie, just to let her know that she's still your pony? On the same basis, Babs can ride Patch. Perhaps you'd like to put them both over our cross-country course.'

'I'd love to.' I glanced at my watch. 'But I'm afraid I can't. I'm due back at Three Paddocks in half-an-hour. I'll take Misty, though, just to let her know she still belongs to me.'

I was about a quarter-of-a-mile from the Stars when I heard a desperate mewing. Reining up, I listened. The sound was thin and plaintive, like a kitten in trouble.

I slid down from the saddle and tied Misty to the nearest gate while I investigated.

The mewing seemed to come from the other side of the hedge. I climbed the gate and dropped down into a field of corn.

'Mew! Miaow! Meee-ow . . ." The cries sounded fainter as though the animal was becoming exhausted. Searching along the hedge bottom I came to a rabbit run. 'Miaow!' The last cry was stronger again.

Parting the long grass I saw a small bundle of spiky fur. Three tabby paws were crouched beneath. The fourth, ending in a short white 'mitten' was extended. There was blood on the 'mitten' and a circle of wire, drawn tight round the paw, had cut into the flesh. The kitten had been caught in a rabbit-snare.

'You poor little thing!'

Gently I stretched my hand to touch between the flattened ears. But the kitten didn't know that I could be trusted. Tugging her trapped paw she turned her head to hiss. Her struggles pulled the wire tighter. There was only one thing to do.

'I'm sorry about this, puss –' I slipped off my anorak and wrapped it round the kitten's small body so that she could not struggle.

Gradually I edged the kitten nearer to the snare to relieve the pressure on her paw. Then, leaning the weight of my body across her to hold her down, I pulled the snare out of the ground. Soon I was able to work the wire loop free. Only then could I see how deeply it had bitten into the kitten's paw.

I gazed at the wound aghast. 'That must hurt a lot, Puss. I'll take you straight to Three Paddocks.'

Barney O'Rorke was a wonder with horses. I hoped his magic might extend also to cats, and I didn't hope in vain. The curly-headed Irish youth knew just what to do. Taking the injured handful of fur from me, he crooned to it lovingly.

'Poor wee thing. 'Tis a terrible time you've had. You're safe now, my darling. Barney will make your paw well again in no time at all.'

The kitten had stopped shivering at his touch. Now she set up a purr as he carried her to the tack-room.

'A bowl of warm water and salt and we'll get that

cleaned up.' He turned to me. 'We'll need some ointment, Jackie. Run to Karen for the key of the first-aid box.'

Ten minutes later, the injured paw was cleaned and dressed and the kitten's pink tongue was dabbing up a saucerful of milk by the tack-room stove.

'Where shall we bed the kitten down, Barney?' Karen came to supervise. 'Shall I put a blanket in a carton and let her stay in the tack-room for the night?'

'No. I've an idea of my own.'

When the kitten had finished lapping Barney picked her up and settled her in the crook of his arm. 'She'll be mortal sleepy now,' he declared. ''Tis a good time to try out my notion.'

With the kitten snuggling drowsily in his arms he carried her towards Colleen's loose-box.

'Not in there,' Karen protested. 'Colleen may have been quieter since you came but I don't think it would be wise to put a kitten in with her.'

Barney was unperturbed. 'There's no need to be worrying yourself, Karen. The mare wouldn't be after hurting such a little creature. Besides I can't stay here for always. I'm hoping that the kitten may make a friend to keep the mare quiet after I've moved on.'

'Oh, Barney! Don't talk about going away!' Karen's eyes were strangely pained. 'We need you here.'

Barney seemed surprised.

Without answering he made a nest for the kitten in the straw in a corner of Colleen's box. When he put the kitten on the ground Colleen lowered her head to blow at it in gentle enquiry. The kitten's ears flattened; then, sensing comfort in the warmth of the big animal's breathing, she settled down to sleep.

I looked up, surprised to see that Karen had moved to Barney's side.

'Don't go, Barney,' she said softly.

I blinked. Was Karen getting a crush on Barney? It wasn't so surprising. After all, Barney was quite good-looking and gently-spoken in his Irish way.

A couple of years ago I might have thought 'how soppy!' but now I sighed: 'Oh, dear!' There might be unhappiness ahead for Karen and that wouldn't improve her temper!

13 *Karen's crush*

Day succeeded happy day . . . and Barney stayed!

Meanwhile, the problem mare became fond of the kitten. The Stars put a notice in the window of the local shop to state that they had found the stray but no one came forward to claim her. She was named Cushla. Her paw quickly improved and soon she was scampering fearlessly between Colleen's feet while the temperamental bay seemed not to mind. In fact, as the kitten grew stronger, Colleen became calmer, just as Barney had intended. Having a stable-companion had helped the mare to settle down.

Barney, too, seemed to be happy. He was busy all day, working with the horses and practising with Karen and Sally for the team. In his spare moments he encouraged me to ride Brigand and coached me over the higher jumps.

'That's the way of it, Jackie. Keep your eye on the middle of the fence. Brigand's not so experienced as your Misty. He needs you to tell him where to take off.'

And again; 'Steady now. You must always approach a big fence slowly. Three strides from take-off – then's the time to increase your pace. Jumping's mostly a matter of timing – slow – slow – quick – quick – quicker – *over!*' He slapped the rhythm on his thigh.

'Come on, Barney.' There was barely a session which Karen did not interrupt. 'What's the use of wasting time coaching Jackie? For goodness sake, let's concentrate on the team.'

Her eyes flashed jealously. She had resented her twin, Dirk, taking an interest in me. She was even more possessive over Barney. Yes, she definitely had a romantic crush on the Irish youth.

'Don't take too much notice of what Barney tells you,' I overheard Dirk warn his twin one evening while we were bedding down the horses. 'You'll only get hurt, Karen. Barney may tell you that you're 'the prettiest rose that ever came from Tralee' but that's just his Irish blarney. He'll have been saying things like that to every girl he's met since he was big enough to groom a pony. After all, what do we really know about him? He's not told us anything about his past.'

'You're just jealous of me having any other friends.' Karen banged down the feed-bucket with an emphasis that made Rowan jump. 'Just because we're twins doesn't mean you own me, Dirk.'

The relationship between the Star twins grew more edgy every day. It came to a climax on the morning of the qualifying Trials.

The Southern Counties' heat was to be held at Summerdown, forty miles away. The horses were to travel there in two boxes. Mr and Mrs Star and

Edmund, who was now home but forbidden to ride, were driving over by car and the rest of us were to share the cabs of the horse-boxes with the drivers.

I had been up since five that morning, helping Babs to prepare Misty. We had washed her tail and plaited her mane the previous evening but there was still plenty to do to ensure that my pony looked her best. Mrs Green had promised to collect Babs and Misty with a pony-trailer and they were due to join the rest of Marston Riding Club Under-Fourteens at the ground.

I rode Patch to Three Paddocks, getting there at twenty to seven. Aware that I was late, I had expected to find the stables in a bustle, the twins and Sally grooming their ponies, Barney mucking out – dashing from one loose-box to another, putting finishing touches here, there and everywhere.

To my amazement the stable yard was deserted. Only the five horsy heads looked out over their half-doors to whicker a greeting to Patch.

Whatever had happened? Had everyone overslept?

Jumping off Patch I ran to the tack-room.

'Hey, Barney! Wake up!' I called up the stairs to the stable flat. 'It's late and the qualifying heats of the Trials are to be held today. Remember?'

There was no reply.

Thinking perhaps that Barney may have been offered the comfort of a bed in the house to enable him to get the best possible night's rest before the competitions, I banged on the Stars' door.

'Hey, wake up, everybody. We're going to be late.'

'Whatever's wrong? What's the time?' Dirk's sleep-tousled dark head was thrust out of one of the windows.

'It's ten to seven,' I yelled.

Dirk jerked from his sleepy state to full alertness as his gaze swept the peaceful yard. 'Where's Barney? Why hasn't he started morning-stables?'

'I don't know. I can't find him.'

'Right!' Dirk said. 'Get started on Brigand, Jackie. I'll waken the others and be down in two shakes.'

I was about to measure out the piebald's feed when I saw a piece of exercise-book paper, folded in half and propped on top of the corn bin. I unfolded the note and read Barney's laboriously written screed.

Sorry – but I shan't be able to ride at Summerdown after all.

I really am a rolling stone and now the time has come when I've got to roll on. Jackie's a good little rider and I've been bringing her on in case I had to go. Let her ride Brigand and take my place in the team.

Tell Karen the memory of the light in her brown eyes will cheer me on my travels.

Wishing you all the luck of the Irish,

Barney.

P.S. I've worked hard in the stables, helped a lot with the schooling and gentled the bay mare for you and I didn't ask any pay. So I hope you won't grudge me the loan of the old bike from the tack room. I borrowed Dirk's old bomber jacket, too. I need something to keep me dry when it rains so I reckon I've more real need for it than him. He can always get his father to stump up for something new and classy.

'Gosh!' I thought as I gazed at the note in disbelief. 'Who'd have dreamt that Barney would let everyone down like this?'

I was still staring at the missive when Dirk arrived followed by Karen and Sally.

'What's this then?' Dirk took the note from my hand and read it aloud. 'Hm! Just as I expected.'

'How can you say that?' Karen turned on her twin, eyes flashing. 'There must be some explanation. Barney must be in trouble.'

'I can well believe that,' Dirk said shortly. 'Probably he's in trouble with the police!'

'Don't be so horrible!' Angrily Karen turned on her twin, beating at his chest with her fists.

Dirk seized her wrists. 'Calm down, Karen, and try to face facts. Respectable people don't suddenly turn up out of thin air the way Barney did – no references, no background, nothing. I'm afraid it looks very much as if he may be on the run.'

'You and your legal mind!' Karen wriggled free from her brother's grasp. 'You're so practical, aren't you? Cynical, too. Always ready to think the worst.'

'Barney didn't come here from *nowhere*, Dirk.' Sally backed up her older sister. 'Babs sent him from Colonel Graham's.'

'She told him to come here because Colonel Graham didn't want him at the Grange,' I said flatly, facing the truth. 'Colonel Graham must have thought like Dirk and decided that, as Barney had no references, he wouldn't be reliable.'

'And if he's not reliable, who cares?' challenged Karen. 'As Barney said in the note, he's done us some good turns. She turned to Dirk, her eyes widened in apprehension. 'You're not going to make a fuss to the police, are you? Can't you forget about that bike and your old bomber jacket? Barney's sure to return them when he gets out of whatever trouble he's in – *if* he is in trouble.'

'Please, Dirk.' Sally tugged at the sleeve of her elder brother's shirt. 'Don't go to the police.'

'If you do,' threatened Karen, 'I'll never forgive you.'

Dirk sighed. 'Oh, very well. I suppose we mustn't think the worst of Barney. He did work without wages, after all.'

'Yes,' nodded Sally, 'all we gave him in return was his meals and a bed.'

14 *A horsy crisis*

Karen was too upset to give her mind to the feeding and grooming of the horses that morning.

She was in a bad temper and most of it was directed at me.

'Jackie, you're hopeless! Can't you bandage Brigand's legs better than that? Don't forget the tail-guard. Anybody would think you've never prepared a horse for travelling to a competition.' She dropped the stable-fork in her annoyance. 'Buck up! Get Brigand into the horse-box with Rowan and help me put up the flap. We're so late that we shan't have time to muck out and leave the stables ready for to-night.'

Karen's edginess continued all the way to Summerdown. We were latish at the ground. In the vehicle park, trailers and horse-boxes were already backed into position. Horses and ponies were being led out and trotted up and down. The early competitors were already walking the course. Across the ground I caught sight of Misty's grey head looking out of the pony trailer behind Mrs Green's yellow Ford.

Babs was among those studying the fourth jump with the rest of the Marston Under-Fourteens. As I watched they disappeared out of sight round the bend of the course.

'For goodness sake stop gawping, Jackie.' Karen's nerves made her more than usually snappy. 'Go to the gate and tell Dirk where we're parked.' She glanced at her watch. 'If he and Sally don't turn up soon we shan't have time to inspect the course. The Under-Fourteens will have started and no one will be allowed on the ground.'

It must only have been a matter of minutes, although it seemed like hours, before the second of the Stars' hired horse-boxes rumbled into the parking ground. Leaving the horses still inside, the four of us went to collect our numbers and then set off to walk the course.

The first three made-up fences did not look too difficult. The fourth had a wide stretch of water in front of a cut-and-laid hedge. Beside it, a television crew was setting up its camera.

'They're expecting trouble here,' Dirk deduced while Sally and I shivered. 'Disaster always makes the most compulsive viewing. Have a good look, all of you. The going's soft after last night's rain. By the time the Under-Fourteens have churned it up, the take-off will be really tricky. I'll go first to pick the safest spot.' He turned to Sally. 'Woodbine may be a bit nappy if we have to jump near the side. Don't let her run out. You'll have to use your legs and drive her on.'

We reached the part of the course which had hitherto been hidden from view. Here there was a choice of obstacles: a formidable-looking bank, a double-oxer with a ditch on the landing side, and a solid wall belonged to the shorter but more difficult circuit. The outer would take longer but had easier obstacles – simple posts-and-rails or brushwood fences.

'Which shall we tackle?' Sally looked anxiously to her older brother.

'We'll take the quickest route, of course,' Dirk told her. 'Our horses are up to the bigger fences and every second will count. Never forget that we shall be riding against the clock.'

Time was our enemy even then. We were not able to complete our course inspection because the bell went to clear the ground for the start of the Under-Fourteens.

Marston was the last to go. By the time it came to the turn of Babs and her team-mates there had already been two rounds with under forty penalties. Most of the obstacles had been lowered for this junior event. Even so, some of them were formidable enough and I wondered how my cousin and Misty would fare as they lined up with Felicity Wayne-Smith, Charles Lang and Bill Quale for the start.

They were away! I watched Misty's hooves drumming purposefully as she neared the first fence.

'Don't waste time, Jackie.' Karen caught at my arm. 'Come on. We've got to get our own mounts ready. It's our class next. Remember?'

As if I could forget! Just the same I had to see Babs and Misty over that fence. They cleared it with the rest of the team and I allowed myself to be led towards the Stars' horse-boxes. Even so, I kept looking back over my shoulder. I'm afraid I wasn't paying much attention to the instructions Karen gave me. I was out there with Misty and Babs, crossing my fingers as they neared each jump. Not until they were out of sight did I accompany Karen into the box to bring out our mounts.

I removed Brigand's tail-guard and unwound the bandages from his legs. Then I put on his bridle and placed his saddle on his back before turning him to lead him out of the box. As I reached the ramp I was again able to see the course. I did not know how Misty and Babs had fared out in the country, but they were now on the home-stretch with the rest of the team galloping towards the parallel bars.

I stopped as they neared the obstacle. 'Watch it, Babs,' I called out. 'Let Misty choose her take-off. She'll need plenty of scope to clear the second pole.'

From behind me Karen's voice rose tensely: 'Jackie, do get on!'

Sensing my excitement Brigand began to jig as I led him on to the ramp. 'Hold hard,' I warned Karen. 'Don't bring Rowan too close!'

The ramp began to quiver under the piebald's shifting feet.

Out there, on the course, Babs and her team-mates were clearing the hog's back. Now there was only the wall! In suspense, my fingers tightened on Brigand's reins. Half off the ramp the piebald paused, dug in his fore-feet and refused to move.

'For heaven's sake, Jackie!' Behind me Karen was unable to check Rowan who, sensing the thrills of the competition ahead, was eager to be out of the box.

The mare's nose touched Brigand's quarters and he lashed out. One of his jumping studs caught Rowan.

'Now you've done it, Jackie!' Karen's wail was anguished as she bent to staunch a sudden flow of blood with her handkerchief. 'Rowan's fore-leg's laid open. It'll need stitching. She won't be able to jump. And it's all your fault!'

15 *Dreams come true*

I felt dreadful about poor Rowan's leg, but there was little I could do. It was up to me and Misty to make amends.

'Is it asking too much of you to tackle the course again, Misty?' I murmured to my pony as I patted her neck. 'Babs has wisped you down well. You look none the worse, even though it was a gruelling round.'

'Misty can do it,' Babs urged. 'She never put a foot wrong with me. We'd have won if it hadn't been for Felicity Wayne-Smith's pony refusing at the water. As it is, our team is out of the championship. You might just as well have the use of Misty for the Under-Eighteens.'

'I suppose I can risk it,' I said doubtfully. 'At least it will give the Stars a chance to compete.' Pulling up Misty's girth, I drew her reins over her head, swung myself into the saddle and trotted her across the field in response to frantic signals from Karen and Sally by the horse-boxes.

Rowan's gash had been stitched and the vet had given her an anti-tetanus injection. Dirk had obtained the judge's permission to substitute Misty for the injured mare. Karen had decided to ride Brigand, leaving me free to pilot my own pony. So far the best round had only twenty penalties. If we could beat that and have no time faults, then we would go through to the finals of the National Championship.

For the Stars' sake I hoped it might be so.

'A lot depends on you and me, Misty,' I bent to whisper near her furry ear. 'It's asking a lot of you, I know. You're only a pony and you'll have to tackle the jumps at hunter-height.'

Three more teams had to compete before it was our turn and all three came to grief. Several riders fell at one or other of the water-jumps. One team had seemed to be doing creditably. Then Babs, who had been deputed to watch the part of the course that was hidden from us, had raced back to report that they had tried to tackle the shorter circuit and that one of the ponies had refused twice at the bank.

'So there's still only one really good round to beat.' She patted Misty. 'Good luck, all of you!'

'Think what a tonic it will be for Edmund,' said Dirk, 'if we manage to go through to the finals.'

'Probably Edmund will be well enough by then to jump.' Karen darted a still-unfriendly glance in my direction. 'Rowan will be fit, too, so I can ride her and Edmund can have Brigand. All four Stars on our own horses – we should be unbeatable! But, of course, there's still this heat to win.' Again she glanced coldly at me. 'Unfortunately, Jackie, we're in your hands.'

'There's nothing unfortunate about it,' Dirk said quickly. I knew he was afraid his twin's words might rattle me so that I did badly on the course. 'We're jolly lucky to have Jackie. As for Misty, if she goes as well for Jackie as she did for Babs, no one will have any cause to complain.'

Then the bell went and we were on the course!

'Don't forget the gate,' Babs yelled after us. 'One of you must open and close it.'

'Already settled,' Karen snapped. Scarcely deigning to acknowledge Babs' good intentions, she glanced at the rest of us. 'Dirk will do it, of course.'

There was a last minute delay while the course-builders put together one of the knocked-down fences. Brigand shifted, fretting his bit. He was raring to go and Karen had to circle him several times to calm him. I took the chance to check Misty's girth and to jam my crash cap even firmer on my head.

At last we were off, Dirk setting the pace.

As we had expected, the first three made-up fences did not give us much trouble. Almost before I had time to think, Dirk galloped slightly ahead and Karen, Sally and I rode abreast as we headed for the first stretch of water, lying menacingly in front of the cut-and-laid hedge. Beside it, the television crew waited hopefully to record more disasters.

As Dirk had expected, the take-off had been badly churned up by the other competitors.

Now he urged Viking on, riding him at the extreme right of the jump, the only spot where our mounts' hooves could be expected to get a grip.

'Let me go in front of you, Jackie,' Sally urged at my

side. 'My only hope of Woodbine not running out is to let her follow Brigand. It'll help her to tackle the water if you and Misty are behind her to drive her on.'

I reined up Misty. Already Dirk was clear of the jump. Behind him Karen clapped her heels to Brigand's sides as he rose in a powerful take-off. Next went Sally. For luck, I crossed two fingers of my right hand on the reins as the youngest Star legged on her brown mare. Mercifully Woodbine followed her stable-companions' lead. They were over without a splash.

Having reined back to let Sally jump, Misty came at the water more slowly than I would have liked. I raised my switch to urge her on. It was unnecessary. Before I could touch her, my pony put in an extra short stride, seeming to gain the impetus she needed.

With a leap that would have done credit to a much bigger animal, she launched herself into the air and cleared the water with a couple of feet to spare.

Next we came to the bank. Here, too, the take-off was bad. I looked ahead to Dirk, wondering whether he would decide to tackle it or whether he would take the easier post-and-rails of the outer circuit. The more difficult jumps made for speed and time was all-important.

As I had expected, Dirk set Viking at the bank. At that moment, Brigand cut across him. In an attempt to 'fly' the bank the powerful piebald landed awkwardly on top. Karen was not one of my favourite people, but I had to admire the way she handled Brigand. Almost by force she got the piebald's head up, preventing him from going down, heeling him over the low hedge and urging him to slither down the far side of the bank.

Behind her, Dirk legged on his chestnut. Then Sally and I urged our mounts on to the bank. Side by side, Woodbine and Misty popped over the hedge, brought their hocks under them and successfully descended the steep slide of the bank.

On again!

I saw Dirk glance at his watch as he rode for the double-oxer. At full gallop, Karen, Sally and I pounded after him. Misty was gallantly keeping up with the bigger horses, but she was sweating heavily and I knew it was asking a great deal of her. This was her second time round the demanding course. The jumps were higher and the pace was hot. Even so, excitement seemed to carry my pony on. We left the oxer and its ditch behind us to sail over the wall. Ahead of us lay the gate. Dirk was already coming up to it. He had it open but I could see that he was having trouble with Viking. The chestnut did not want to wait. Already we were pounding down on him. Viking tossed his head, impatient to be off, to keep his lead.

'Can you take over and close the gate, Karen?' Dirk shouted to his twin as he let the chestnut have his way.

'Can't stop!' Karen gasped, shooting through the gateway almost on the heels of her brother's mount.

'Jackie! What are we going to do?' Sally gave me a startled glance as Misty thundered along beside Woodbine. 'This mare's hopeless at gates. I'll never get it shut.'

'Leave it to me.' I hoped hard that, in the excitement, Misty's commonsense would not desert her.

Our luck held. I had the gate closed, and now I was legging Misty after the other three as they rode for the parallel poles. Some specks of mud left Woodbine's heels to strike me in the eyes. As we took off I could hardly see.

We were over and I wiped the mud away. We were going so fast that we were on the second water-jump almost before I realised it and I was nearly left behind. Misty's take-off threw me forward. I was on her neck as we landed but my clever pony seemed to hesitate just a second – long enough for me to regain the saddle – and then we were off again, riding for the hog's back. We were over and clear. Now there was only the final wall.

Ahead, Viking took it well, so did Brigand and Woodbine. Now there was only Misty and me. If we could jump the height without dislodging the lath on top we would achieve the coveted best round.

We made it!

Now it was only a question of beating the clock. Crouching over Misty's neck, I put her into a full gallop for the finish. Froth from her bit flecked my cheek as, neck extended, she propelled herself after the other three. We were almost level with Sally and Karen as the finishing bell rang.

Babs scrambled through the rails and ran towards us.

'Seven seconds faster than Southdown B., only four penalties and no other teams to go,' she told us.

Dirk gave an undignified whoop as the judge's announcement over the tannoy confirmed that we were indeed the winners.

Only one thing marred the joy of our triumph.

From the corner of my eye I saw a rangy figure in a faded bomber jacket disappearing into the crowd.

'Barney!' Karen called. She handed Brigand's reins to Dirk and, ducking under the rails, ran after the Irish youth.

'Leave him alone, you idiot!' Dirk called after her. 'Can't you understand he didn't want us to see him?'

Karen did not heed her brother's bidding. Already she was pushing her way through the crowd.

'Ah, well!' Dirk sighed. 'Karen must learn her own lessons, I suppose. Barney will soon be fed up with her bossy ways. Come on, the rest of you. Let's get these horses watered and rubbed down.'

Babs took over Brigand, working on him beside Misty and me. Dirk and Sally saw to Viking and Woodbine. We were wisping busily when Karen made her way back to us some ten minutes later.

'Any luck?' asked Sally.

Karen shook her head.

'Couldn't you find Barney?' Babs impulsively disregarded my nudge to keep quiet.

'As a matter of fact I did.' Karen's face was pink and she looked near to tears. 'I spoke to him all right! But he didn't want to know me.'

'But why?' puzzled Sally. 'I thought you and he were special friends.'

'So did I!' Karen made a play of helping Babs put on Brigand's anti-sweat rug.

Dirk left Viking to lay a hand on his twin's shoulder. 'What happened?'

'Evidently Barney didn't want to be recognised,' Karen said. 'He asked me what I thought I was doing, drawing attention to him.'

'Perhaps the police *are* looking for him, then,' I said.

Karen shook her head. 'It was the horses Barney came to see. Before he dodged into the crowd he said I needn't flatter myself thinking he'd come to see me. It was just the Irishman in him that made him want to watch the horses that he'd helped to train.'

Dirk sighed. 'Barney thinks more of horses than of people, I dare say. You'll survive, twin. He wasn't right for you. He'll probably always be unstable: a pity when he has such a way with animals.' He touched Karen's shoulder. 'I had a word with Colonel Graham about him last night. The Colonel said the reason he didn't take on Barney at the Grange was because he'd been warned about him by a friend. Apparently Barney had worked in the friend's stables for six weeks. Then he left with twenty pounds and a saddle that didn't belong to him.'

'Rather like our own experience,' Karen's voice was wistful.

'Yes.' Dirk nodded. 'Mind you, we're partly to blame, not paying him any wages.'

'That gave Barney some excuse, I suppose, to make off with the bike and bomber jacket.' Karen was quiet for a moment while the rest of us – a bit embarrassed – looked at her sympathetically. She brushed a hand across her eyes and took Rowan's bridle to lead the mare into the horse-box. 'I suppose it's all to do with growing up. People aren't always what they seem at first sight.' She patted her mare's neck. 'Thank goodness horses are easier to understand.'

Halfway up the ramp Karen stopped and turned to me. 'It's my own fault I suppose for being beastly to you, Jackie. If I hadn't been so keen to get you out of the team I might not have been so ready to make a hero of Barney. I've been an idiot.' She looked embarrassed. 'And I've misjudged you.'

'I should think so,' Dirk agreed. 'We Stars owe everything to Jackie and Misty. Without them we wouldn't be through to the finals.'

It was my turn to feel uncomfortable. 'Think no more about it.' The memory of my own jealousy and its consequences came into my mind as I looked across at Babs. 'Events have a way of upsetting one's judgment.'

'Anyway, Jackie, I'm sorry.' Karen led Rowan on into the horse-box. A moment later she appeared at the top of the ramp. 'I hope you won't let the way I've treated you make any difference. You and Babs are welcome at Three Paddocks any time.'

'Of course they are,' said Dirk. 'What would we do without them?'

'You won't need us,' I said slowly. 'Once Edmund is back in the saddle, you'll have your own family team again.'

'We shall still need a reserve,' assured Dirk, firmly.

'And a *reserve* reserve,' Karen smiled. 'Once Babs has reached her fourteenth birthday she'll qualify for that. Meanwhile we won't have to let either of you get rusty. We shall expect to see you and your ponies at Three Paddocks at least twice a week for the rest of the holidays.'

Super, I thought happily. Babs and me, Misty, Patch and the Jumping Stars . . . Once it would have seemed unbelievable. I'd never dreamt that I'd be invited to help in the Three Paddocks stables – much less to have ridden as a member of the Stars' team.

It seemed after all that, with a little luck, even the wildest of pony dreams could sometimes come true!